MEAT

MEAT

PERFECTLY PREPARED TO ENJOY EVERY DAY

This edition published in 2012

LOVE FOOD is an imprint of Parragon Books Ltd

Parragon
Chartist House
15–17 Trim Street
Bath, BA1 1HA, UK

www.parragon.com/lovefood

ISBN: 978-1-78186-725-9

Printed in China

Concept: Patrik Jaros & Günter Beer
Recipes and food styling: Patrik Jaros www.foodlook.com
Text: Günter Beer, Gerhard von Richthofen, Patrik Jaros, Jörg Zipprick
Photography: Günter Beer www.beerfoto.com
Photographer's assistants: Sigurd Buchberger, Aranxa Alvarez
Cook's assistants: Magnus Thelen, Johannes von Bemberg
Designed by Estudio Merino www.estudiomerino.com
Produced by Buenavista Studio s.l. www.buenavistastudio.com
The visual index is a registered design of Buenavista Studio s.l. (European Trademark Office number 000252796-001)
Project management: trans texas publishing, Cologne
Typesetting: Nazire Ergün, Cologne

Notes for the Reader
This book uses standard kitchen measuring spoons and cups. All spoon and cup measurements are level unless otherwise indicated. Unless otherwise stated, milk is assumed to be whole, butter is assumed to be salted, eggs are large, individual vegetables are medium, and pepper is freshly ground black pepper. Unless otherwise stated, all root vegetables should be washed and peeled before using.

For the best results, use a meat thermometer when cooking meat and poultry—check the latest USDA government guidelines for current advice.

Garnishes and serving suggestions are all optional and not necessarily included in the recipe ingredients or method. The times given are only an approximate guide. Preparation times differ according to the techniques used by different people and the cooking times may also vary from those given. Optional ingredients, variations, or serving suggestions have not been included in the calculations.

Recipes using raw or very lightly cooked eggs should be avoided by infants, the elderly, pregnant women, and people with weakened immune systems. Pregnant and breast-feeding women are advised to avoid eating peanuts and peanut products. People with nut allergies should be aware that some of the prepared ingredients used in the recipes in this book may contain nuts. Always check the packaging before use.

Picture acknowledgments
All photos by Günter Beer, Barcelona

Contents

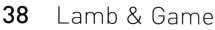

Introduction

Meat—a staple food

Do we need meat? No, not really, as millions of perfectly healthy vegetarians prove. And yet most of us find it far easier to eat healthily if we include meat in our diets. Meat contains many valuable nutrients needed by the human body that are present only in a limited or inferior form in plant products. To compensate for this, and to be sure their diet is not lacking in any valuable substances, vegetarians have to combine different vegetable dishes.

Above all, meat is the principal source of the valuable protein we need for our immune systems, digestion, and blood clotting, the transportation of nutrients, muscle and bone development, and for our hair, nails, and skin. Just 3½ ounces of meat provides an average of ¾ ounce protein. Animal protein is processed better by the human body than plant protein because it is very similar in composition to human body protein.

Meat is also an important source of vitamins B_1, B_2, B_6, and B_{12}, which regulate our metabolism, and vitamin A, which is good for our eyes, as well as vitamin D, which we need for our bones and teeth. Pork is an especially good source of vitamin B_1, whereas vitamin B_{12} is present, above all, in beef. Meat is also

the best source of iron, which is more readily absorbed from animal sources than from vegetables. Meat also contains the trace element selenium and plenty of zinc. Like iron, zinc from animal products is absorbed more easily than from vegetable products.

To maintain a healthy eating plan, it's important that meat—like all foods—is of a good quality and that it's eaten in reasonable quantities. A maximum of three portions (5½ ounces each) of lean meat is the recommended consumption per person per week.

Apart from its health-related benefits, meat also has the advantage of being prepared in an abundance of ways and flavors. Virtually no other type of food is as versatile. Meat can be marinated, stuffed or coated, boiled, fried, broiled, grilled, or oven-roasted, and served with a multitude of herbs and spices. It can be used in small quantities in sauces for pasta and noodle dishes. Combined with vegetable products, meat dishes guarantee us a balanced and, above all, varied diet.

Meat quality

Always look for meat that has been properly produced—this can be more expensive than meat and poultry that

has been intensively reared, but it will be tastier and more nutritious. The following five criteria will help you check the quality of meat:

- Smell: Fresh raw meat should have a neutral to slightly acidic smell.
- Moisture content: Fresh, high-quality meat does not lose much water, so it should be almost dry, or moist only on the surface. Do not buy soft, oozing meat that is already lying in its own juice on the butcher's counter.
- Consistency: Meat should be firm to the touch, not spongy. If you press your finger on it, it shouldn't leave a mark.
- Color: Fresh beef has a distinctive dark red color, lamb is pale red to red. Pork should be pale pink and bright and shiny. Game, on the other hand, should be reddish to dark brown. Chicken is a light meat, and the skin and meat of corn-fed poultry are yellowish in color. Duck is darker but should never be grayish green.
- Fine marbling: The marbling pattern in meat is caused by streaks of fat in the muscle tissue. This fat content intensifies the meat's flavor during cooking. However, fatty meat is not good for your health in the long term.

Storing meat

Unpack meat from the retail packaging immediately after purchasing, wrap it in aluminum foil, and store in the coldest part of the refrigerator. Frozen meat or poultry should be thawed in the refrigerator with a plate or bowl under it to collect the drips. Thawed meat should be cooked within one day of thawing and, to be on the safe side, it should be cooked through.

Let leftover cooked meat cool before storing it in the refrigerator. Never keep fresh meat in the refrigerator for longer than four days. If possible, ground meat and variety meats should be prepared on the day of purchase.

Meat in the kitchen

Always wash your hands with hot water before and after handling meat. Thoroughly clean the sink and all equipment used to prepare or thaw meat after use. Use a separate cutting board that can be washed with hot water. Raw meat or melted water from frozen meat should not be in contact with other foods, especially if this food won't be heated.

When reheating meat dishes, using a meat thermometer, make sure the temperature of the meat reaches at least 170°F for poultry and 160°F for other meats. Only temperatures above this destroy the majority of pathogenic germs, such as salmonella.

Preparation

There are no set rules for cooking meat because each type of meat and cut requires a different type of preparation. Leaner pieces are often sautéed, grilled, or broiled, while fattier, tougher pieces tend to be boiled or stewed. Finer pieces of lamb or beef should be cooked so that they are still pink inside. However, this is a matter of taste, and some people always prefer well-done meat. Any type of ground meat, as well as pork, chicken, and turkey, should always be well cooked. The following chapters contain detailed information about cooking and roasting times and recipes for all types of meat preparation so that you can find the methods that you like best.

How to use this book

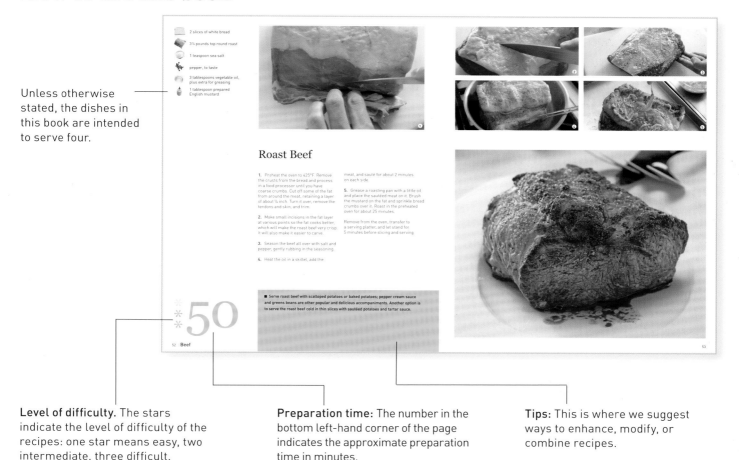

Unless otherwise stated, the dishes in this book are intended to serve four.

Level of difficulty. The stars indicate the level of difficulty of the recipes: one star means easy, two intermediate, three difficult.

Preparation time: The number in the bottom left-hand corner of the page indicates the approximate preparation time in minutes.

Tips: This is where we suggest ways to enhance, modify, or combine recipes.

How to Cut Up Poultry

1. Remove the foot sections with a knife. Place the bird on a clean work surface, legs pointing toward you.

2. Pull the legs away from the body and cut to the bone with a knife.

3. Break the legs off at the joints and turn the bird over.

4. Remove the thumb-size fillets and cut off the drumsticks.

5. Make an incision around the wing, about 1¼ inches from the breast, then scrape off the meat to the wing tip to expose the bone. Separate the wing with the back of the knife.

6. Carefully move the skin up to avoid damaging it and loosen the wishbone with the tip of the knife.

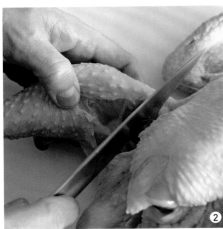

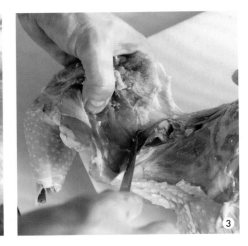

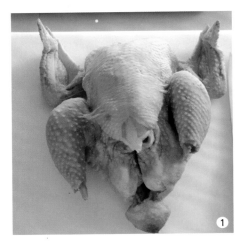

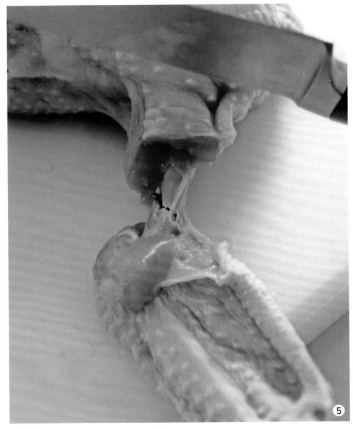

7. Carefully remove the wishbone. This will make it easier to cut out the breast around the chest. Otherwise, you would have to cut around the wishbone, which takes a lot of practice.

8. Make an incision along the breastbone from where the wishbone was removed and cut from the abdominal cavity to the neck.

9. Use your hand to pull back the breast and cut in such a way that the wing bone remains attached to it.

10. Continue the process for the other breast, drumstick, and wing. Use the bones for soups or sauces.

■ You can prepare the liver and kidneys separately and serve them, for example, as an appetizer with mâche.

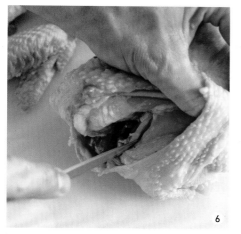

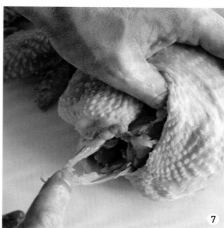

4 (6-ounce) skinless chicken breasts

 salt and pepper, to taste

 4 slices cooked ham

 2 slices Gouda cheese, Gruyère cheese, or Swiss cheese

 ¾ cup all-purpose flour

 2 eggs

 2 cups dried bread crumbs

 ⅓ cup vegetable oil

 1 tablespoon butter

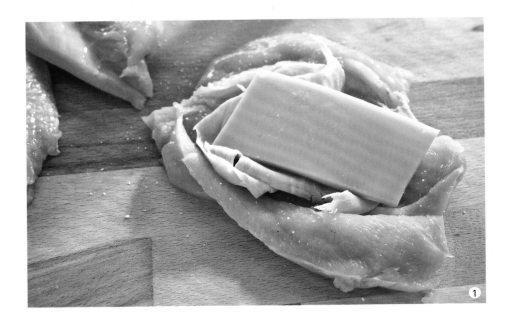

Chicken Cordon Bleu

1. Cut a pocket lengthwise into each chicken breast. Season the breasts on both sides with salt and pepper and fill each pocket with a slice of ham and half a slice of cheese.

2. Fold the chicken breast over, enveloping the ham and cheese.

3. Seal any open spots and press the meat down a little.

4. Put the flour in a shallow dish and dip the breasts in the flour to coat, shaking off any excess. Beat the eggs in a bowl, then dip the floured chicken breasts in the beaten egg. Put the bread crumbs in a shallow dish and dip the chicken breasts in them to coat.

5. Heat the oil and butter in a skillet over medium heat, add the chicken breasts and cook on each side for about 7 minutes.

Serve immediately.

■ To make the meat even more tender and tasty, marinate the cut chicken breasts for 2 hours in some plain yogurt mixed with a pinch of cayenne pepper.

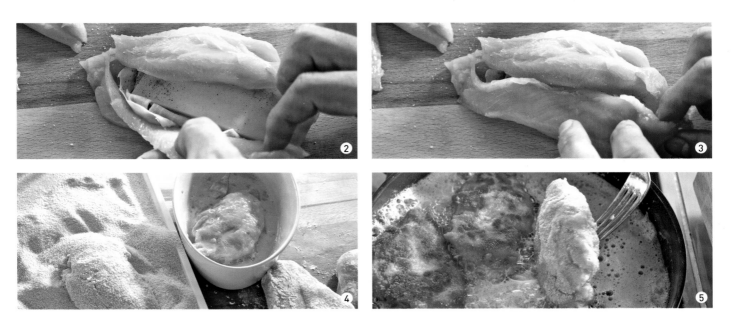

4 (6-ounce) skinless chicken breasts

 salt and pepper, to taste

 2 eggs

 dash mineral water

 ¾ cup all-purpose flour

 4 cups dried bread crumbs

 ⅓ cup vegetable oil

1 tablespoon butter

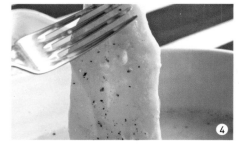

Traditional Chicken Schnitzels

1. Remove any fat or gristle from the chicken breasts. Season on both sides with salt and pepper.

2. Break the eggs into a shallow dish, season with pepper, and beat in the mineral water using a fork.

3. Put the flour in a shallow dish, then place the chicken breasts in the dish and dust with the flour on both sides, shaking off any excess.

4. Dip the chicken breasts in the egg until they are completely covered.

5. Put the bread crumbs into a shallow dish, then dip the chicken breasts in the bread crumbs to coat.

6. Heat the oil and butter in a skillet.

7. Place the schnitzels in the skillet and sauté in the oil-and-butter mixture.

8. Shake the skillet gently so that the fat covers the chicken. This will make sure that the meat gets cooked on the top.

9. After about 5 minutes, turn the schnitzels over and sauté for an additional 5 minutes. Keep shaking the skillet so the batter becomes really crisp.

10. Remove the schnitzels from the skillet and drain on paper towels.

Arrange on serving plates and serve with a cucumber salad and lemon wedges for squeezing over the chicken.

■ You can bring a little zing to this recipe by adding 1 teaspoon of dry English mustard to the flour.

* *
* 20
* *

2 fresh rosemary sprigs,
plus extra to garnish

 2 fresh thyme sprigs

 1 whole chicken

 salt and pepper, to taste

 1 egg

 1 tablespoon all-purpose flour

 2¾ slices of white bread

 3 tablespoons olive oil

Baked Chicken with a Herb Crust

1. Preheat the oven to 400°F. Finely chop the rosemary and thyme. Cut up the chicken and put the pieces on a cutting board. Cut the breast twice. Separate the legs at the joint and cut through the upper part along the bone. Season with salt and pepper.

2. Beat the egg in a mixing bowl. Add the flour, rosemary, thyme, and some salt. Mix with a fork and work into a batter. Cut the crusts off the bread and process to fine crumbs in a food processor. Dip the chicken pieces in the egg mixture. Add the bread crumbs and mix.

3. Place the chicken pieces on a baking pan and drizzle with the oil. You may have to cover the chicken with aluminum foil to prevent the herb crust from burning. Cook in the preheated oven for about 20 minutes, until a meat thermometer reads 160°F, or until the juices run clear when you pierce the thickest part of the chicken with the tip of a sharp knife.

Arrange the chicken in a serving dish, garnish with rosemary sprigs and lemon wedges, and serve.

■ To achieve a good crust consistency, you must use really fresh bread crumbs. Store-bought bread crumbs are far too dry and will result in a hard crust.

1 garlic bulb

 1 lemon

 bunch fresh parsley

 4 (12-ounce) Cornish game hens

 salt and pepper, to taste

 4 small onions

 4 tablespoons butter

Cornish Game Hens Roasted with Lemon & Garlic

1. Preheat the oven to 350°F. Set the garlic, stem upright, on a work surface and press down with the palm of your hand to loosen the cloves. Remove the outer skin and crush the cloves in their skins. Rinse the lemon under hot water and cut into ¼-inch slices. Pluck the parsley leaves off the stems. Wash the Cornish game hens and dry them inside with paper towels.

2. Thoroughly season the hens, inside and out, with salt and pepper. Stuff with the crushed garlic cloves and the parsley, reserving some of the parsley to garnish.

3. Place the stuffed hens in a roasting pan. Cut off the stem end of the onions but do not peel. Arrange the onions and lemon slices around the hens. Distribute the butter evenly over the hens.

4. Roast for 25 minutes in the preheated oven. Add ½ cup of water to the pan and scrape the bottom with a wooden spoon to loosen the sediment. Baste the hens with the juices and roast for an additional 15 minutes. Remove from the oven.

Garnish the hens with the reserved parsley and serve with the onions and juices.

✳✳✳ 80

■ Be careful not to injure the skin when you pluck the remaining pinfeathers with fishbone pliers. The white meat would dry out at these spots. Cornish game hens taste just as delicious cold. Serve with any type of potato dish.

6 sticks butter

 6 eggs

 1½ teaspoons dried marjoram

 salt and pepper, to taste

 ½ teaspoon freshly grated nutmeg

 8 ounces poultry livers

 18 slices of white bread, thickly sliced

 1¼ cups heavy cream

 13–15-pound turkey, with giblets

 5 carrots

 3 onions

 3 celery stalks

 1 cup apple cider or apple juice

 3 cups chicken stock or water

 2 fresh thyme sprigs

Turkey with Bread Stuffing

1. To make the stuffing, beat the butter at room temperature in a large mixing bowl until creamy. Add 1 egg, and the marjoram, season with salt and pepper, and continue to beat until the egg is completely mixed in. Add the grated nutmeg, then mix in the remaining eggs, one at a time.

2. Cut the liver into thin slices and combine with the butter mixture.

3. Cut the bread, including the crust, into ½-inch cubes and put into a mixing bowl. Pour the cream over the bread cubes and let soak for about 10 minutes.

4. Carefully mix everything together with a wooden spoon so that the bread cubes retain as much of their shape as possible.

5. Preheat the oven to 300°F. Clean the turkey cavity well and remove the giblets. Season generously with salt and pepper inside and out. Stuff the turkey with the bread stuffing, but make sure that the filling does not come out at the neck.

6. Tie the turkey with string and place in a roasting pan. Cut the carrots, onions, and celery into 2-inch pieces.

+ 5 hours' slow cooking

60

■ You can add cooked chestnuts, steamed apples, dried apricots, or pieces of sautéed pumpkin to the stuffing. Served with sweet potatoes and cranberry sauce, it makes the perfect Thanksgiving dinner.

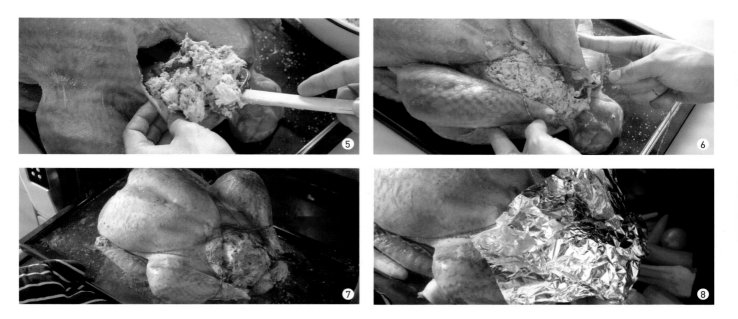

7. Pour the cider over the turkey and roast in the preheated oven for 4 hours, basting from time to time with the juices. You can thin the juices by adding some of the stock from time to time.

8. After 4 hours, lay the thyme and the vegetables around the turkey. Cover the stuffing with aluminum foil and pour 2 cups of the stock into the pan. Roast for an additional 1 hour, turning over the vegetables occasionally. Remove them from the juices and place them in a saucepan. Pour the juices through a strainer and reserve.

Place the turkey on a cutting board and serve with the juices and the vegetables.

4 (7-ounce) duck breasts

 2 oranges

 salt and pepper, to taste

 1 tablespoon vegetable oil

 ½ cup Cointreau

 1 cup orange juice

2 tablespoons pickled green peppercorns

Roasted Duck Breast with Orange-Pepper Sauce

1. Place the duck breasts on a cutting board, skin-side up. Cut off the protruding skin. Using a sharp knife, cut the skin in a crisscross pattern.

2. Grate the orange peel using a fine grater. Use a knife to cut off all the pith from the orange, then slice the orange.

3. Season the duck breast on both sides with salt and pepper. Heat the oil in a skillet and place the breasts in it, skin-side down.

4. Cook the breasts over medium heat for about 10 minutes on each side, basting frequently with the duck fat. Continue to cook on the skin side until the skin is very crisp.

5. Arrange the duck breasts, skin-side up, on a serving platter and let stand. Remove the fat from the skillet, place the orange peel in it, and add the Cointreau to the juices. Add the orange juice, pepper-corns, and orange slices.

Serve the duck breasts on warm plates with the orange-pepper sauce.

■ Score the skin deeply to make sure that the fat escapes, otherwise the skin won't be very crisp.

2½ cups dried pinto beans

 1 large carrot

 2 celery stalks

 2 garlic cloves

 1 small onion

 2 tablespoons olive oil

 4 fresh rosemary sprigs

 3 bay leaves

 1 teaspoon fennel seeds, chopped

 1 tablespoon tomato paste

 1 cup white wine

 salt and pepper, to taste

 9 cups chicken stock

 2 (7-ounce) duck breasts

①

Pinto Bean Ragout with Roasted Duck Breast

1. Soak the beans for at least 5 hours. Cut the carrots and celery into ¼-inch pieces. Crush the garlic cloves into a bowl, then dice the onions. Heat the oil in a shallow saucepan, then add the onions, carrots, and celery and gently sauté for 10 minutes.

2. Add the rosemary, bay leaves, fennel seeds, and garlic and lightly sauté.

3. Push the vegetables to one side of the pan. Add the tomato paste to the center of the pan so it loses its acidity. Add the wine, letting the liquid reduce.

4. Drain and rinse the beans, add to the pan, and sauté for 2 minutes. Season with salt and pepper, then pour in the chicken stock and simmer gently for 50 minutes. Stir occasionally to prevent the beans from sticking to the bottom of the pan. Stir carefully to avoid crushing them. Add a little water if necessary.

Meanwhile, cook the duck breasts (see page 20). Divide the beans between four serving plates, then slice the duck breasts, arrange on top of the beans, and serve immediately.

+ 5 hours' soaking

80

■ Fennel seeds are easier to chop if you drizzle them with a little oil beforehand to prevent them from jumping. The pinto bean ragout also goes well with sausages.

Types of Pork Cut

The hallmarks of good pork are an almost ivory white, odorless, firm meat without moistness. It's not necessarily a bad sign if a piece of pork has two different colors. This can be due to the fact that a butcher made a cut at a crucial place, or it can indicate the stress levels of the pig before it was slaughtered.

Pork tastes best when it comes from free-range farms. This is particularly the case if the animals were fed on acorns and chestnuts.

The meat of intensively factory-farmed pigs usually proves to be disappointing: their flesh is watery and they have enormous chops and hams. The flavor will be poor because the characteristic fat has been bred out.

There are hardly any reliable signs of quality. Nevertheless, when buying pork, you should make sure that it is dry and is not exuding any liquid. Meat that turns grey quickly also comes from intensively farmed pigs in the industrial sector.

For best results, the fat should be removed only after the pork has been roasted or stewed; it's an important flavor enhancer. If the pork has been wrapped in paper by your butcher, it will keep for about two days in your refrigerator at a temperature of 36°F.

In France, there is a well-known saying: *Tout est bon dans le cochon*; everything on a pig is good. Indeed, expert butchers know how to make full use of this animal. The blood is used in blood sausages and the intestines are made into sausage casings. The breast meat can be smoked or cured.

The belly and the neck have far more fat than cutlets; that, however, is not a disadvantage. As already said, fat is an important flavor enhancer. These cuts are inexpensive and lend themselves to long slow cooking, and are ideal for using in casseroles, stews, and other substantial winter dishes.

Cooking Chart

Product	Weight	Method	Temperature	Time	Note
Roasted pork with crackling (cut into the crackling with a razor blade)	4 pounds	Oven	350°F	100 minutes	
Rolled pork belly	3¼ pounds	Oven	325°F	110 minutes	
Smoked pork roast, uncooked	3½ pounds	Oven	300°F	70 minutes	
Pork tenderloin medallions	2¼ ounces	Skillet	Medium heat	8 minutes	
Ground pork	4½ pounds	Oven	325°F	80 minutes	
Suckling pig leg	5–6 pounds	Oven	325°F	90 minutes	
Goulash	Large cubes	Saucepan with lid	Low heat	70 minutes' stewing	20 minutes' gentle sautéeing
Knuckle of pork	2½ pounds	Oven	350°F	80 minutes	
Spareribs	2¼ pounds	Oven	325°F	40 minutes	
Ground pork meatballs	1 pound	Oven	350°F	25 minutes	
Pork chops	8 ounces	Skillet	Medium heat	6 minutes	
Pork shoulder cuts	10 ounces	Skillet	Medium heat	10 minutes	

Pork tenderloin

Pork chop

Roast pork

Pork shoulder

Ham hocks

Ground pork

Suckling pig leg

Spareribs

Pork belly for a rolled pork roast

Ribs

Pig's foot

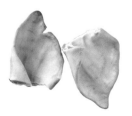

Pig's ears

salt, to taste

 1 onion, studded with cloves

 2 carrots

 ¼ head of celeriac

 1–2 suckling pig legs

 1 pineapple

 1 tablespoon cloves

 3 tablespoons honey

 pinch of cinnamon

 2 tablespoons vegetable oil

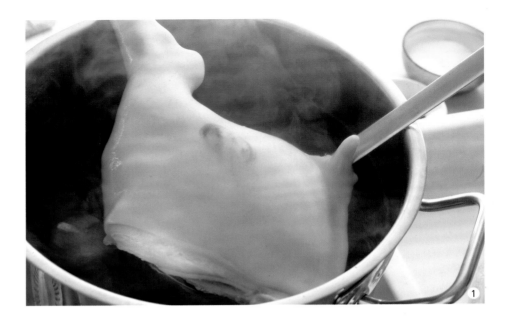

Suckling Pig Leg with Honey & Pineapple

1. Preheat the oven to 325°F. Bring a large saucepan of lightly salted water to a boil. Add the onion, carrots, and celeriac. Add the pig legs and simmer for 5 minutes. Remove the pan from the heat. Remove the legs and let them cool on a cutting board. Reserve the pan juices.

2. Score the skin with a very sharp knife every ½ inch. Cut the skin off the pineapple, cut it into ½-inch-thick slices and set aside. Stick the cloves into the meat. This will give a wonderful flavor to the dish.

3. Put the meat into an ovenproof dish and drizzle with the honey. Roast in the preheated oven for 1½ hours, basting frequently with the pan juices. Lightly season the pineapple slices with salt, dust with cinnamon, and rub with oil. Put them into a ridged grill pan and sear them for 1 minute on each side.

Arrange the pineapple slices on plates with the pig legs on top and serve drizzled with the roasting juices.

180

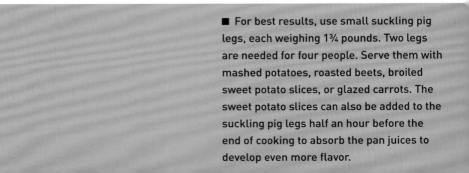

■ For best results, use small suckling pig legs, each weighing 1¾ pounds. Two legs are needed for four people. Serve them with mashed potatoes, roasted beets, broiled sweet potato slices, or glazed carrots. The sweet potato slices can also be added to the suckling pig legs half an hour before the end of cooking to absorb the pan juices to develop even more flavor.

2 ripe pears

 1 tablespoon butter

 1 tablespoon sugar

 pepper, to taste

 2 fresh thyme sprigs, plus extra to garnish

 4 (5-ounce) pork shoulder cutlets

 salt, to taste

 1 tablespoon vegetable oil

4 ounces Gorgonzola cheese or other blue cheese

Pork Cutlets Baked with Pears & Gorgonzola Cheese

1. Peel, halve, and core the pears. Cut lengthwise into segments.

2. Melt the butter with the sugar in a skillet. Add the pear segments, season with pepper, and add the thyme, then toss until the mixture is slightly caramelized.

3. Season the pork with salt and pepper. Heat the oil in a nonstick skillet, then add the cutlets and sear on both sides. Transfer them to a baking dish.

4. Preheat the broiler to high. Lay the pear segments on top of the cutlets.

5. Put the cheese on top of the pear segments, place under the preheated broiler, and cook for 2–3 minutes.

Arrange the cutlets on plates and pour the pan juices over them. Garnish with thyme sprigs and serve immediately.

■ You can use dried fruit, such as plums, apples, or apricots, cooked in red wine instead of pears.

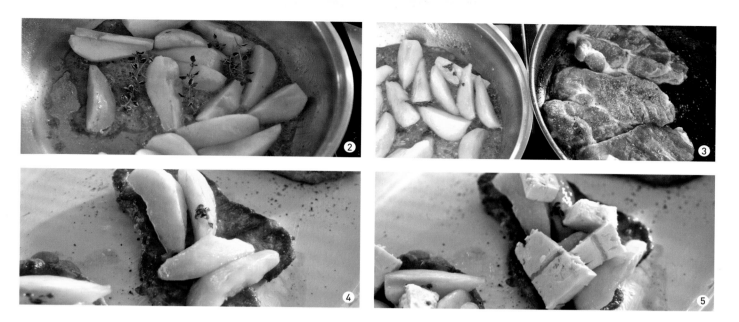

1 pound ground pork

 2 tablespoons oyster sauce

 1¾ cups canned coconut milk

 1 teaspoon red curry paste

 1 (11-ounce) can corn kernels, drained

 2 tablespoons slivered almonds

Pork Meatballs Cooked in a Coconut-Curry Sauce

1. Preheat the oven to 350°F. Mix the pork with the oyster sauce and shape into small balls. Put them into a shallow ovenproof dish. Pour the coconut milk into a tall container.

2. Add the curry paste to the coconut milk and stir.

3. Using an immersion blender, blend the mixture briefly, until the curry paste is thoroughly mixed in.

4. Pour the sauce over the meatballs. Sprinkle with the corn kernels, followed by the slivered almonds. Cook in the preheated oven for about 25 minutes, covered with aluminum foil to prevent the slivered almonds from burning.

Transfer the meatballs to bowls and serve immediately.

 45

■ Milder yellow curry paste can be used instead of the red curry paste. A few young green peas can be added to the sauce too.

1-inch piece fresh ginger

 ½ teaspoon red curry paste

 ¼ cup oyster sauce

 3 tablespoons vegetable oil

 1¾ pounds pork belly

 1 lime, cut into quarters

Grilled Pork Belly with an Asian Marinade

1. Peel the ginger and finely grate into a bowl.

2. Add the curry paste.

3. Pour in the oyster sauce.

4. Add the oil and stir well.

5. Slice the pork and put it into a plastic container. Pour the marinade over and mix well. Marinate the meat for at least 1 hour, so that the spices can flavor the meat properly. Heat a ridged grill pan over high heat, add the pork slices, and cook on each side for about 5 minutes.

Sprinkle the meat with the juice from the quartered lime and serve immediately.

■ You can also marinate pork chops or pork shoulder in this mixture and then cook in a ridged grill pan or under the broiler.

1 ripe mango

 2 oranges

 1 white onion

 4 tablespoons butter

 1 tablespoon honey

 6 green peppercorn clusters

 salt, to taste

 1¼ pounds pork tenderloin

 2 tablespoons vegetable oil

 pepper

fresh Thai basil leaves, to garnish

Pork Tenderloin with Mango Sauce, Basil & Green Peppercorns

1. Peel the mango, remove the fruit from the pit with a knife, and chop into ¼-inch cubes. Using a vegetable peeler, pare a strip of zest from 1 orange and finely chop. Squeeze the oranges and set aside the juice. Finely dice the onion. Melt 3 tablespoons of the butter in a saucepan. Add the diced onion and gently sauté until it is translucent, then add the mango cubes.

2. Add the orange zest and honey and gently sauté for an additional 5 minutes.

3. Strip the green peppercorns from two of the clusters, reserving the remaining clusters to garnish. Add the peppercorns and the orange juice to the sauce, season with salt, and simmer for about

10 minutes. Meanwhile, cut the pork tenderloin into eight medallions.

4. Add the oil and remaining butter to a nonstick skillet and heat until foaming. Season the pork medallions on both sides with salt and pepper and add them to the skillet. Cook on each side for about 5 minutes, basting with the pan juices from time to time.

Divide the mango sauce among four serving plates and lay two medallions on top. Garnish each serving with a green pepper cluster and some Thai basil leaves.

■ You can replace half of the mango with pineapple when you are preparing the mango sauce, which will taste even fruitier. You can also use curry powder, ginger, or chiles to season it more intensely.

1 (7-ounce) can Mexican salsa

 pepper, to taste

 2 tablespoons fresh rosemary

 8 (5-ounce) pork chops

 2 tablespoons olive oil

 salt, to taste

Grilled Pork Chops with a Mexican Marinade

1. Put the salsa in a bowl.

2. Add some pepper and the rosemary.

3. Put the pork chops on a platter and pour the marinade over the meat.

4. Turn the chops and brush the other side with the marinade. Drizzle a little oil over the chops.

5. Cover the chops with plastic wrap and let marinate in the refrigerator for at least 1 hour and up to 4 hours. Heat a ridged grill pan over high heat, add the chops, and chargrill on each side for about 3 minutes or until cooked through. Season with salt.

Serve the chops immediately with chargrilled green bell peppers.

80

■ Buy a large piece of pork tenderloin and cut it into 1¼-inch cubes. Thread the cubes of pork onto skewers, alternating them with pieces of green bell pepper and sliced onion, and season them with the marinade. Cook slowly on a ridged grill pan or under a broiler.

Types of Lamb & Game

Lamb: Good lamb is pink with a snowy white, solid layer of fat. This fat layer should be firm to the touch. If you are allowed to touch the meat, warm your hands first before sliding them over the fat layer. If the lamb is too old, your fingers will subsequently have the distinctive, pungent smell of mutton. A dull red, almost purple, or downright black color is a bad sign. This kind of meat also comes from older animals and tastes like mutton. You should also be careful with regard to large chops or cutlets. A normal lamb weighs 30–33 pounds. Anything heavier than 40 pounds is classified as mutton. Female animals are tastier than male. Lamb can be stored in the chill compartment of the refrigerator at 32–36°F for two days.

In order to enjoy really good game, you need to know or be a hunter. However, some types of traditionally "wild animals" are also farm-raised nowadays.

Hare: Female hares taste better than their male counterparts. The males are tougher and more solid. The lighter the color of the meat, the younger the animal. A red to a reddish black color is a sign of an old, tough hare. Young hare is more tender and is suitable for roasting. Older animals are better suited to marinating and slow cooking methods, such as stews and casseroles.

Venison: Males have dark, almost brown meat, whereas the meat of females is somewhat paler. The smaller the animal, the lighter and more delicate its meat. As with lamb, female animals taste better than their male counterparts.

Cooking Chart

Product	Weight	Method	Temperature	Time	Notes
Leg of lamb	3¼ pounds–4 pounds	Oven	350°F	100 minutes	
Lamb liver	10½ ounces	Skillet	Medium heat	2 minutes	Cut into ½-inch slices
Rack of lamb	1 pound	Oven	325°F	20 minutes	
Lamb chop	2 ounces	Ridged grill pan	Medium heat	5 minutes	Rub the chop with oil in advance, so that it doesn't stick to the grill pan
Lamb cutlet	2 ounces	Skillet	Medium heat	4 minutes	
Shoulder of lamb	3 pound–3¼ pounds	Oven	400°F	45 minutes	
Saddle of venison	Whole, 4½ pounds	Oven	350°F	35 minutes	Sear on all sides, in advance
Roast venison (female)	2½ pounds–3¼ pounds	Oven	325°F	45 minutes	
Knuckle of lamb	9–10 ounces	Oven	325°F	90 minutes	
Roast venison (male)	4½ pounds	Oven	325°F	70 minutes	
Venison medallion	2 ounces	Skillet	Medium heat	10 minutes	
Haunch of venison	2¼ pounds	Oven	350°F	25 minutes	
Rabbit	3 pounds	Oven	325°F	40 minutes	
Rack of hare	1 pound	Oven	350°F	20 minutes	
Leg of hare	14 ounces	Saucepan with lid	Medium heat	70 minutes	
Leg of rabbit	9 ounces	Skillet with lid	Medium heat	30 minutes	Stew

Leg of venison

Venison medallions

Haunch of venison

Rack of lamb

Lamb chop

Leg of lamb

Rack of hare

Rabbit

Loin of venison

½ cup olive oil

 2 tablespoons fresh thyme

 1 tablespoon fresh rosemary

 1 teaspoon fennel seeds

 salt and pepper, to taste

 4-pound leg of lamb, plus some lamb bones

 1 garlic bulb

Roasted Leg of Lamb with Herbs & Garlic

1. Preheat the oven to 400°F. To make the marinade, pour the oil into a bowl and add the thyme.

2. Coarsely chop the rosemary and add to the bowl with the fennel seeds. Mix well and season with salt and pepper.

3. Put the lamb into a roasting pan with the bones and rub the meat all over with the herbed oil. Separate the garlic cloves from the bulb, place them in a bowl, and press down on them lightly with the heel of your hand. Put the garlic cloves on top of the leg of lamb.

4. Put the lamb in the preheated oven and roast for 30 minutes. Turn the roast frequently and baste it with its juices. Reduce the oven temperature to 350°F and roast for an additional hour. While the lamb is roasting, add some water to the pan from time to time and use a wooden spoon to scrape the sediment from the bottom of the pan to make a sauce.

Arrange the leg of lamb on a platter. Remove the bones from the sauce. Pour the sauce over the lamb and serve.

100

■ Finely chop tarragon, marjoram, parsley, and lemon and orange zest and mix them with butter. Add to a skillet, heat until foaming, and pour the foam over the cooked lamb.

 2 (2¼ pound) racks of lamb

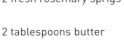 salt and pepper, to taste

3 tablespoons olive oil

6 garlic cloves

2 fresh rosemary sprigs

2 tablespoons butter

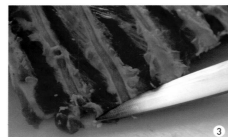

Roasted Rack of Lamb with Rosemary

1. Put the racks of lamb on a cutting board and cut into the skin under the loin at a depth of ½ inch.

2. Trim the skin and the meat from the ribs.

3. Shave the skin off the bone with the knife, so that it is easier to remove.

4. Carefully loosen the skin from the bone with your fingers, until the bone is exposed and clean.

5. Turn it over and cut this part of the skin off.

6. Cut along the backbone and remove the white sinew carefully. Then continue cutting on the back to the ribs.

7. Turn it over again and separate the rack of lamb from the backbone with sharp kitchen shears.

8. Remove the small pieces of sinew and bones from the separated rack of lamb and season it with salt and pepper on both sides.

*
60
*
*

■ You can use prepared racks of lamb. The rack of lamb can also be roasted with a pecan-lemon marinade. Coarsely chop some pecan nuts, cut 2 pieces of lemon zest into fine strips, and mix with 1 fresh rosemary sprig, 2 tablespoons of olive oil, and 1 teaspoon of whole-grain mustard. Roast the lamb with this mixture for the last 5 minutes of cooking. Scalloped potatoes and green beans are very good accompaniments for rack of lamb.

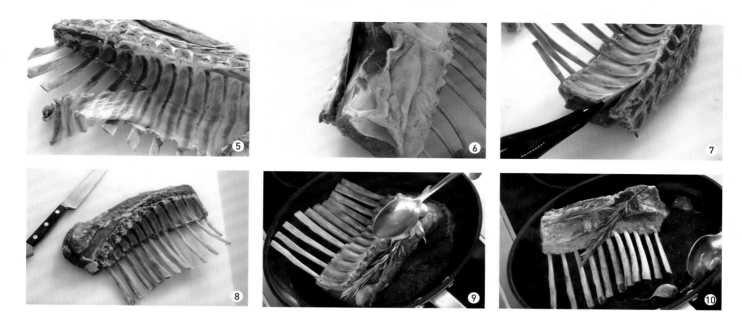

9. Preheat the oven to 350°F. Heat the oil in a wide, ovenproof skillet and put the rack of lamb in it top-side down. Place the unpeeled garlic cloves in a bowl and press down on them with the heel of your hand. Add the garlic and the rosemary to the rack. Baste the lamb with the pan juices and turn it over after 5 minutes, replacing the rosemary on top of the rack so that it doesn't burn in the pan.

10. Add the butter and roast in the preheated oven for about 10 minutes, basting frequently.

Remove from the oven, cover with foil, and let rest for 3 minutes before serving.

3-pound leg of lamb

 bunch fresh parsley

 1 fresh tarragon sprig

 5 shallots

 2 large carrots

 3 onions

 1 small head cabbage

 2 garlic cloves

 3 Yukon gold potatoes

 2 tablespoons vegetable oil

 salt and pepper, to taste

 ½ teaspoon tomato paste

 1 bay leaf

5 cups beef stock

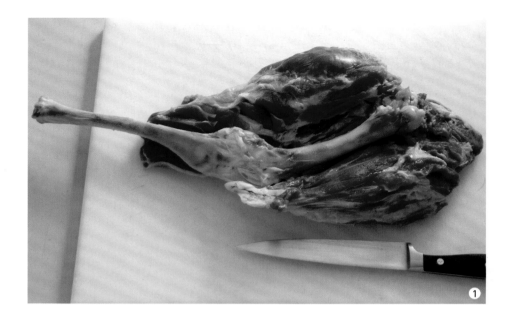

Irish Stew with Cabbage & Carrots

1. Cut into the leg of lamb along the bone and remove it carefully from the meat with the tip of your knife. Remove the fat and gristle from the skin. Cut the meat into 1¼-inch pieces. Pluck the the leaves from the parsley and tarragon sprigs and set aside. They will be chopped shortly before they are added to the dish in order to preserve their flavor and their essential oils.

2. Cut the shallots in half. Cut the carrots diagonally into ½-inch thick slices. Halve the onions and cut them into strips. Remove the outer leaves from the cabbage, cut it in half, remove the stem, and cut it into 1¼-inch cubes. Peel the garlic and finely chop. Peel the potatoes and cut into 1¼-inch cubes.

3. Heat the oil in a saucepan, add the garlic and then the onion strips, and cook until they are translucent. Season the meat with salt and pepper, add to the pan, and gently sauté for 10 minutes. Push the meat to the side, add the tomato paste to the center of the pan to brown it a little, then mix it with the meat. Add the bay leaf.

4. Pour the stock over the meat. You can use water as a substitute, but you will need to season the meat more if you do. Bring the stew to a boil, then simmer, covered, for 15 minutes.

■ Lamb shoulder can be used instead of leg of lamb, but it will have to be cooked for 15 minutes longer, because it is more marbled. The quantity of vegetables can be increased or other vegetables used according to your preference. Green beans, celery, and Savoy cabbage are every bit as delicious in this stew.

5. Add the carrots, shallots, and potatoes and simmer, covered, for an additional 10 minutes. Add the cabbage, mix together all of the ingredients, and simmer for an additional 20 minutes, then remove the bay leaf.

Finely chop the parsley and the tarragon, stir them into the pan, then serve the stew in soup bowls.

4 rabbit haunches

salt and pepper, to taste

1 tablespoon sweet paprika

2 small onions

2 tablespoons butter

2 cups chicken stock or
vegetable stock

1¾ cups cream

Stewed Rabbit in Paprika Cream Sauce

1. Season the rabbit haunches with salt and pepper and dust with paprika.

2. Finely dice the onions. Melt the butter in a wide saucepan over low heat. Add the onions and gently sauté until they are translucent. Add the rabbit haunches and lightly brown.

3. Add the stock, bring to a boil, then cover, reduce the heat, and cook for about 30 minutes.

4. Turn the rabbit occasionally. You may have to add some water if the liquid evaporates quickly. The bottom of the pan should always be covered with a ½-inch layer of liquid.

5. Add the cream and simmer the rabbit in the sauce. You may need to add more salt and pepper to season the stew.

Serve with boiled potatoes or noodles.

■ A whole, cut-up rabbit can be prepared in the same manner. If you omit the paprika and add 4 cups of sliced button mushrooms after you brown the rabbit, you will have a wonderful mushroom sauce.

45

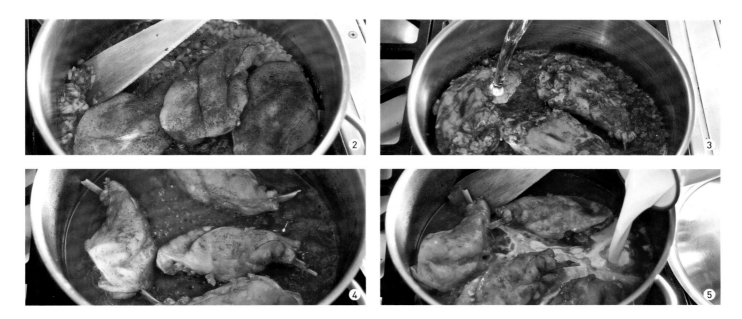

1 cup bacon fat

 2 (14-ounce) racks of hare

 4 pears

 salt and pepper, to taste

 ¼ cup vegetable oil

 10 juniper berries

 5 bay leaves

 2 fresh rosemary sprigs

 3 tablespoons butter

 1 tablespoon packed light brown sugar

 2 tablespoons cranberry jelly

Rack of Hare with Cranberry Pears

1. Put the bacon fat in the freezer for half an hour or so. This makes it easier to handle. Remove the skin and the membrane from both racks of hare. Cut the bacon fat into strips 2 inches long and ¼ inch thick. Grip a strip of fat in the back end of a larding needle.

2. Carefully stick the point of the needle into the meat and guide it through until the bacon fat is evenly distributed in the rack and is protruding slightly. Repeat every ¾ inch. Larding makes the meat juicier.

3. Peel the pears, cut them in half, and remove the core with a melon baller. Leave the stem on the pear to make it more visually attractive.

4. Preheat the oven to 350°F. Season the meat with salt and pepper. Heat the oil in a skillet, add both racks, and sear on one side, then turn them over. Transfer to a roasting pan. Crush the juniper berries, add them to the pan with the bay leaves, then lay the rosemary sprigs on top of the hare. Roast in the preheated oven for approximately 20 minutes, basting frequently with the pan juices.

■ For best results, use small Bartlett pears. Serve the rack of hare accompanied by small potato cakes, noodles, or a mushroom cream sauce.

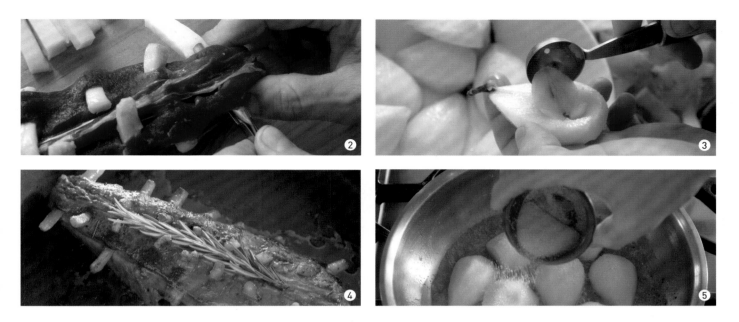

5. Meanwhile, melt the butter in a skillet and sprinkle in half the sugar. Lay the pear halves in the skillet cut-side down. Sprinkle with the remaining sugar and slowly sauté until they are golden yellow. Turn the pear halves over and fill them with the cranberry jelly.

Pour the pan juices over the meat, transfer to a platter, and serve with the pears. To serve, remove the hare meat from the racks with a knife and cut diagonally into ¾-inch-thick slices.

Degrees of Cooking for Beef

Beef tenderloin steak

Rare/blue: The meat is sautéed for 1 minute on each side and is raw on the inside.

Medium rare/saignant/bloody: The meat is sautéed for 3 minutes on each side and has a pink center with a bloody core.

Medium/pink: The meat is sautéed for 5 minutes on each side and remains pink on the inside. However, the core is no longer bloody.

Medium well/à point/half done: The meat is sautéed for 6 minutes on each side and is slightly pink on the inside. However, there are no bloody juices when cut.

Well done/bien cuit: The meat is sautéed for 8 minutes on each side and is well done on the inside. There are no juices when cut.

2 slices of white bread

 3¼ pounds top round roast

 1 teaspoon sea salt

 pepper, to taste

 3 tablespoons vegetable oil, plus extra for greasing

 1 tablespoon prepared English mustard

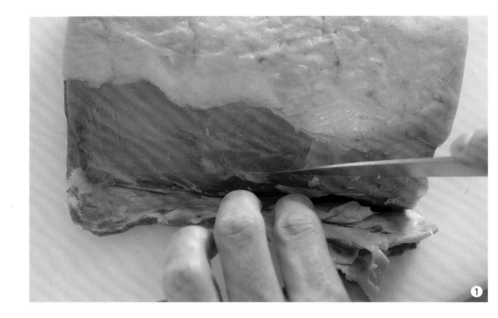

Roast Beef

1. Preheat the oven to 425°F. Remove the crusts from the bread and process in a food processor until you have coarse crumbs. Cut off some of the fat from around the meat, retaining a layer of about ¼ inch. Turn it over, remove the tendons and skin, and trim.

2. Make small incisions in the fat layer at various points so the fat cooks better, which will make the roast beef very crisp. It will also make it easier to carve.

3. Season the beef all over with salt and pepper, gently rubbing in the seasoning.

4. Heat the oil in a skillet, add the meat, and sauté for about 2 minutes on each side.

5. Grease a roasting pan with a little oil and place the sautéed meat on it. Brush the mustard on the fat and sprinkle bread crumbs over it. Roast in the preheated oven for about 25 minutes.

Remove from the oven, transfer to a serving platter, and let stand for 5 minutes before slicing and serving.

■ Serve roast beef with scalloped potatoes or baked potatoes; pepper cream sauce and greens beans are other popular and delicious accompaniments. Another option is to serve the roast beef cold in thin slices with sautéed potatoes and tartar sauce.

5 juniper berries

 5 white peppercorns

 2 onions

 3 carrots

 2 leeks

 4 celery sticks

 1 tablespoon coarse sea salt

 2¼ pounds beef round

 2 cloves

 1 bay leaf

 fresh flat-leaf parsley, to garnish

snipped fresh chives, to garnish

1

Beef Stew with Root Vegetables & Herbs

1. Using the flat side of a knife, lightly crush the juniper berries and peppercorns.

2. Halve the unpeeled onions and cut off the root ends. Halve the carrots. Cut the leeks and celery sticks into two or three pieces, depending on their size.

3. Bring a large saucepan of lightly salted water to a boil, add the beef, bring back to a boil, and simmer for about 1 hour.

4. Add the vegetables and spices and simmer for an additional 1 hour.

5. Season with salt and pepper and stir.

Cut the vegetables into bite-size pieces and arrange them on a serving platter with the beef. Sprinkle over some parsley and chives and serve.

✳ ✳ ✳ **120**

■ Serve with parsley potatoes, sautéed potatoes, or creamed spinach. This dish tastes delicious with tartar sauce.

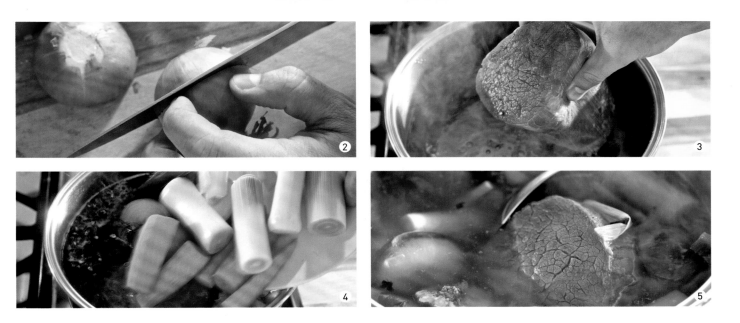

2 large carrots

1 head broccoli romanesco or broccoli

1½ cups green beans

10 asparagus spears

2 tablespoons coarse sea salt

⅔ cup peas

½ bunch fresh chives

2½ cups beef stock

1¾ pounds tenderloin steak

salt and pepper, to taste

1 stick cold butter

freshly grated nutmeg, to taste

Tenderloin Steak in Chive Broth with Spring Vegetables

1. Cut the carrots into 2-inch pieces. Cut the romanesco into small florets. Trim the green beans. Peel the asparagus and cut into 2-inch pieces. Bring a large saucepan of lightly salted water to a boil. Add the carrots and green beans, then add the romanesco and asparagus and, finally, the peas. Cook until all the vegetables are tender but still firm to the bite.

2. Meanwhile, prepare a bowl of cold water and ice cubes to cool the cooked vegetables quickly and stop the cooking process. Remove the cooked vegetables from the pan with a slotted spoon and plunge in the iced water.

3. Pour the stock into a separate saucepan, bring to a boil, and simmer for 5 minutes. Prepare the tenderloin steak and cut into eight equal portions. Season with salt and pepper and place in the stock. Take the pan off the heat and let stand for 6 minutes. Remove the steak, transfer to a plate, and cover with aluminum foil to keep warm.

■ Serve with fresh white bread, parsley potatoes or steamed rice.

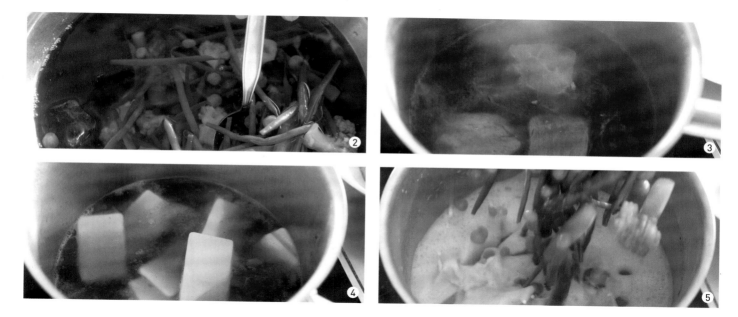

4. Slice the butter, add to the stock, and bring to a boil. Use a whisk to thoroughly blend the butter into the mixture. Add the chives and season with salt and pepper and nutmeg.

5. Drain the vegetables, then add them to the broth and reheat.

Arrange the vegetables in deep soup bowls, place the steak on top, and serve.

1½ pounds fresh ground beef

 1 large onion, finely chopped

 4 small day-old white bread rolls

 2 cups milk

 2 eggs

 2 teaspoons sweet paprika

 salt and pepper, to taste

 1 teaspoon dried marjoram

 1 tablespoon prepared English mustard

 1 teaspoon cornstarch, mixed with a little water

Meatloaf with Sauce

1. Preheat the oven to 375°F and grease a baking dish. Place the beef in a bowl and add the onion.

2. Soak the bread rolls in a shallow dish containing the milk and 2 cups of water for 20 minutes.

3. Squeeze the liquid from the bread rolls and combine them with the eggs, paprika, marjoram, and mustard, and add this to the beef mixture. Mix well and season with salt and pepper.

4. Place the mixture into the prepared baking dish and smooth the top with moistened hands.

5. Cook in the preheated oven for about 1 hour. Occasionally pour some water over the meatloaf. Remove the meatloaf from the dish and cut into thick slices. Add the cornstarch-and-water mixture to the sauce and stir over low heat until thickened.

Pour the sauce over the slices of meatloaf. Serve with parsley potatoes.

■ Add a dash of fresh heavy cream to your sauce. It tastes delicious and it stretches the sauce, just in case you have more company for dinner than expected!

1/3 cup vegetable oil

 3 cinnamon sticks

 8 black cardamom pods

 1 tablespoon black mustard seeds

 1/2 teaspoon star anise seeds

 1 tablespoon ground turmeric

 4 onions

 3 garlic cloves

 2 1/4 pounds shoulder of beef

 salt and pepper, to taste

 1 tablespoon raw brown sugar

 1 (14 1/2-ounce) can peeled tomatoes

3 bay leaves

Indian Beef Curry with Black Cardamom & Cinnamon

1. Heat the oil in a skillet. Add the cinnamon sticks, cardamom pods, mustard seeds, star anise seeds, and turmeric. Lightly toast to intensify the flavor of the spices.

2. Cut the onions into eight pieces each and peel and chop the garlic. Add the mixture to the skillet and lightly sauté.

3. Cut the beef into 1 1/4-inch cubes and season with salt and pepper and the raw sugar. Place the meat in the skillet and sauté for 5 minutes.

4. Add the tomatoes and their can juices, and the bay leaves. Cover the skillet and gently simmer for about 50 minutes, adding some water from time to time.

Serve with the toasted spices and some steamed long-grain rice.

■ Create an Indian curry paste with the following ingredients: 3 red chile peppers, 5 ounces shallots, 5 garlic cloves, 1/2-inch piece galangal, 1/2-inch piece fresh ginger, 1/2-inch piece fresh turmeric root (or use 1 teaspoon of ground turmeric), 2 tablespoons of coriander seeds, 1/2 teaspoon of star anise seeds, 5 cloves, 1/2 teaspoon of fennel seeds, and 1 lemongrass stalk. First, grind the solid spices in a mortar. Add the other ingredients one by one until you have a paste. Use with fish, poultry, or vegetables. Store in glass jars or freeze.

4 onions

 2 tablespoons sugar

 1 bay leaf

 salt and pepper, to taste

 ½ cup wine vinegar

 1¾ pounds lean ground beef

 2 tablespoons oil

 8 lettuce leaves

 2 tomatoes

 2 pickles

 4 soft sesame-seed hamburger buns

 4 teaspoons mayonnaise

 1 tablespoon medium–hot mustard

 4 teaspoons ketchup

Traditional Hamburgers with Onion Relish

1. Halve and thinly slice the onions. Combine them with the sugar, bay leaf, and vinegar, season with salt and pepper, and place in a skillet. Add 1 cup of water and simmer for 25 minutes. The relish is cooked as soon as the liquid is completely reduced and the mixture has a jam-like consistency. Remove and discard the bay leaf.

2. Form four equal beef patties. Heat the oil in a nonstick skillet and place the patties in it. Season with salt and pepper and sauté for about 2 minutes.

3. Turn the patties over. Season again with salt and pepper and sauté for an additional 2 minutes.

4. Slice the tomatoes and pickles. Cut the buns in half and toast them. Put mayonnaise on the bottom half of each bun. Place a lettuce leaf on top and add a burger. Brush some mustard on the burger.

5. Add some tomato slices and top with the onion relish.

Place the pickle slices on top, add some ketchup, then top with the other halves of the buns and serve immediately.

■ Hamburgers are best served with fresh homemade fries. You can use other spicy sauces, cooked bacon strips, or fresh onion rings. If you like, add a slice of cheese of your choice, such as American, Swiss, cheddar, or Monterey Jack, to make a cheeseburger.

INDEX